COMPLETING THE CIRCLE

Anne Stevenson was born in Cambridge, England, in 1933, of American parents, and grew up in New England and Michigan. She studied music, European literature and history at the University of Michigan, returning later to read English and publishing the first critical study of Elizabeth Bishop. After several transatlantic switches, she settled in Britain in 1964, and has since lived in Cambridge, Scotland, Oxford, the Welsh Borders and latterly in North Wales and Durham.

She has held many literary fellowships, and was the inaugural winner of Britain's biggest literary prize, the Northern Rock Foundation Writer's Award, in 2002. In 2007 she was awarded three major prizes in the US: the $200,000 Lannan Lifetime Achievement Award for Poetry by the Lannan Foundation of Santa Fe, a Neglected Masters Award from the Poetry Foundation of Chicago and The Aiken Taylor Award in Modern American Poetry from *The Sewanee Review* in Tennessee. In 2008, The Library of America published *Anne Stevenson: Selected Poems*, edited by Andrew Motion, in conjunction with the Neglected Masters Award. This series is exclusively devoted to the greatest figures in American literature.

As well as her numerous collections of poetry, Anne Stevenson has published a biography of Sylvia Plath (1989), a book of essays, *Between the Iceberg and the Ship* (1998), and two critical studies of Elizabeth Bishop's work, most recently *Five Looks at Elizabeth Bishop* (Bloodaxe Books, 2006). Her latest poetry books are *Poems 1955-2005* (2005), *Stone Milk* (2007), *Astonishment* (2012) and *Completing the Circle* (2020), all from Bloodaxe.

In 2016 she gave the Newcastle/Bloodaxe Poetry Lectures, published by Bloodaxe in 2017 as *About Poems and how poems are not about*.

ANNE STEVENSON

Completing
the Circle

BLOODAXE BOOKS

ISBN: 978 1 78037 498 7

First published 2020 by
Bloodaxe Books Ltd,
Eastburn,
South Park,
Hexham,
Northumberland NE46 1BS.

www.bloodaxebooks.com
For further information about Bloodaxe titles
please visit our website and join our mailing list
or write to the above address for a catalogue

Supported using public funding by
**ARTS COUNCIL
ENGLAND**

Cover design: Neil Astley & Pamela Robertson-Pearce.

Printed in Great Britain by Bell & Bain Limited, Glasgow, Scotland, on
acid-free paper sourced from mills with FSC chain of custody certification.

Per Carla Buranello e Sandro Montesi
Lido di Venezia,
con affetto e grazie infinite

CONTENTS

III

Preface

My title for this collection was originally *Elegies and Celebrations* – unexciting but accurate, for it describes it exactly. Its range of forms and styles is, for me, even more than usually mixed. You will find here among a frequency of sonnets, lyrics, meditations and narratives, a number of light or occasional verses, which may suggest that the book has little purpose other than to please my ear and satisfy my urge to record my experience and remember my friends. The truth is more complicated.

Writing poems in my eighties during the early decades of a newly transformed, already terrifying century, I look back on my disappearing past from the viewpoint of a bewildered survivor. From the first sonnet, 'Anaesthesia', to the last one, 'At 85', these poems cannot help facing up to the realities of time passing and beloved contemporaries dying. The title poem was written over ten years ago after the too-early death of a talented writer who was a close friend of my sister-in-law. It was re-written a year or two later when that sister-in-law herself died. As so often when one suddenly confronts the actuality of death, an (unjust) sense of its arbitrary injustice compelled me to write the poem without knowing where it came from or what it meant. It obviously owes something to Rilke, with whose *Duino Elegies* I was preoccupied at the time. But essentially, like many of these poems, it surprised me by expressing feelings I could articulate only in images, a belief I didn't know I had that death, however personally resented or resisted, in the end has to be recognised and accepted as the complement of life.

Despite its being such a gallimaufry of themes, forms and approaches, I like to think this collection is consistent in maintaining a tone that is serious without being funereal, acquiescent without indulging in confessional despair. In many ways, what we call tone is the most difficult element of poetry to establish without giving way either to imitation or forced originality. My aim – articulated in *terza rima* in 'How Poems Arrive' – is almost always to allow any poem I find myself wrestling with, to tell me finally what it means. Painful feelings need to be loosened by detachment and sometimes lightened by wit. Memories can be better understood when shorn of self-pity and given a context in a larger reality. Personal and impersonal subjects must be treated with the same attention to the way they will sound when read aloud. Getting the tone of a poem right is even more important than getting its rhythm and sounds right; or rather, a poem's tone so much depends on how its sounds and rhythms are deployed that it can take weeks to settle into a final version. The nine lines of 'Candles', for instance, went through over twenty drafts, yet I'm still not sure that all that stitching and unstitching has produced the desired combination of spiritual concern and irony.

The two long narratives placed in section III may seem an anomaly. They really belong in a book of their own, and if five or six years ago I had been able to plunder my experience for more memories of a similar kind, they would have gone into a separate collection. Instead, once these stories were written I ran into a huge barrier of self-doubt. What were they, anyway, prose or poetry? Were they fragments of actual autobiography, or were they invented spin-offs from what once may have happened? I wrote them in free verse; then I wrote them in near blank verse; then I wrote them in prose. Finally I put them away until one day I was looking for poems to send to the editors of *The Hudson Review* and chose 'Pronunciation'. Later I sent them 'Mississippi', though I guessed it might be considered racially controversial, and I didn't expect them to take it. Nor did they. Both narratives have been repeatedly revised. I now defend them as 'poetry' because neither converted happily to prose no matter how stubbornly I tried to persuade them.

Finally, I hope the shifts of mood and subject-matter that characterise these poems will be understood as part of the process of ageing. Wallace Stevens suggested in his memorable study, *The Necessary Angel*, that poetry might be defined as a 'process of the personality of the poet'. That is to say with Marianne Moore that 'poetry is after all personal', that it relates essentially to a poet's prolonged exploration of a life's experience and at its most genuine is neither a matter of competitive opportunity nor of academic dispute. It is at the same time an art that sets the poet at a remove from natural selfishness, so that the satisfaction of successfully completing even the most minor poem becomes, for a few hours, its own priceless reward. 'There! I did it! I finally got it right!' is one of the most pleasurable feelings I know. The craving for sympathetic understanding, for communication, for praise, comes later, along with the doubts. And then, with age, comes the recognition that these verbal footprints that have seemed so important and maybe cost so much emotionally to leave in the sands of what one day will be the past have fulfilled their purpose only if they have contributed in a very small way to a much more vital and impersonal human inheritance. In the end, art has to triumph over experience or all will be lost. It is up to the emerging creators of the coming generation, future artists, future poets – even in the present technological desert, under pressure of climate change and disastrous political leadership – to see that it does.

ANNE STEVENSON
27 October 2019

Saying the World

The way you say the world is what you get.
What's more, you haven't time to change or choose.
The words swim out and pin you in their net

Before you guess you're in a TV set
Lit up and sizzling with unfriendly news.
The word machine – and you depend on it –

Reels out the formulas you have to fit,
The ritual syllables you need to use
To charm the world and not be crushed by it.

This cluttered motorway, that screaming jet,
Those living skeletons whose eyes accuse –
O eyes and ears, don't let your tongue forget

The world is vaster than the alphabet,
And profligate, and meaner than the muse.
A jewel in the universe? Or shit?

Whichever way, you say the world you get,
Though what there is is always there to lose.
No crimson name redeems the poisoned rose.
The absolute's irrelevant. And yet...

(Revised, 21 April 2018)

I

Anaesthesia

They slip away who never said goodbye,
My vintage friends so long depended on
To warm deep levels of my memory.
And if I cared for them, care has to learn
How to grieve sparingly and not to cry.
Age is an exercise in unconcern,
An anaesthetic, lest the misery
Of fresh departures make the final one
Unwelcome. There's a white indemnity
That with the first frost tamps the garden down.
There's nothing we can do but let it be.
And now this *you* and now that *she* is gone,
There's less and less of me that needs to die.
Nor do those vacant spaces terrify.

Poppy Day

Red cross for mercy,
Red flower for remembrance,
The cenotaph wreathed,
The dead – dead, as before.

The great and the good, they
Gather to perform, easing the strain
Of communal conscience;
Somewhere, elsewhere, a war.

White dove of peace,
White flower for *thou shalt not*,
White flag for innocence.
Show the white feather and be shot.

*

They went over the top in the snow,
They really did, and then the snow
Stained red – red as your paper poppy.
They do it again once a year, in November,
Each ghost with a poppy for a gun,
Each somebody's son who fell out of life
For the sake of a maybe future
And a name scratched on stone.

*

If I choose to wear a white poppy,
It might be the opium poppy –
White seed of Asia, *Papaver somniferum*,
Whiteout of sleep, white banner of truce, white
Hope for the mercy of forgetting.
This habit of ceremony and bowed heads
Stands for the red badge of courage.

      *

Stand in the chill of the present and close your eyes.
Unspeakable, the colours of yesterday
Fade into level grey – like language, like memory.
Oh, slippery memory, have you nothing to say
But *sorry, sorry, it was a just war?*
Or was it just a war, televised nightly? Iraq,
Afghanistan, Gaza, far away, black as Rwanda.

      *

Is the overmuchness of us
Too heavy to hang on the cross?
Upright red for the killer in us,
Horizontal white for the kindness in us,
The figure of a question crucified
In the crooked shape of our bodies;
A bowed head praying...or is it sobbing?

Sandi Russell Sings

To Sandi Russell at 70

The darkness, the wetness, the wrongness
    of this English winter –
unwelcome as daybreak's midnight.
    Yesterday's downpour
   is predicting tomorrow's rain.

O friend and forever American,
    what are we doing here, cramped on this island?
How did we fumblingly find our way
    to this teapot of terrible weather?

Exiles or escapists, we have packed the sun
    into our childhoods –
sash windows carelessly opened
    to a soft breeze
scented with hopscotch and roses,

balconies of birthday parties,
    ice-cream sodas,
hot tar on the hot streets melting
    like black snow
under Fourth of July fireworks,
    the flags and the bunting,
the ticker tape parades
    of an always fabulous life.

America the Beautiful, we sang,
    pledging allegiance to the flags
on the Normandy beaches
    and the icon of Iwo Jima.

Do children still sing to their country
        under the school guns?
I remember, I remember how
every day was something to be
        celebrated, something
glorious to wish for, something to grow up for.

Even now, birthdays are a file of screen doors
        through which
a dusty road glimmers in summer sunshine.
        Rain and more rain.
Press your nose to the screen and find your song
        still singing.
The only tale worth telling is the truth
        of what happened.

(Sandi Russell, jazz singer, 1946–2017)

Defeating the Gloom Monster

Remembering Lee Harwood, 1939–2015

After your life died and your work lived on,
you moved from a rented flat in possibility
into more permanent lodgings all your own.
So many rooms, so many habitable poems, each
with a view of a movable city, days sweeping over it,
mountains behind, and a red sun setting fire
to an abstract of evening, suspended and controlled
by a palette of articulate desire.

A naked sensibility clothed lightly in learning;
just what appeared before your eyes
ought to have been enough. But then
there were all those other worlds you had to open
keyed into notes and quotations,
fantasy places you wanted to visit,
never places you wanted to live:
the sultan's palace, the blue mosque, the white room,
a sea of battleships, a sea of glass,
a cattle ranch in Argentina, the passionate grass of Kansas,
an ultra clear blue sky
over the golden hills and vales of a floating continent –
the ever possible geography of love.

They seemed so solid, the dreams, the memories
pouring in unfinished to keep you 'perky' and alert,
hand-holds and toe-holds, a chancy route up
to an always invisible summit in the clouds.

*

Cwm Nantcol. Evening. A restless wind. Boulder clouds
rolling from the West over pearl and rose strata of a calm sunset.
Wish you were here to share the pleasure of it –
the hills assembling their giant silhouettes,
black purples of outcrops and spindly thorn trees,
a scree   a skull   a cliff   an open mouth.
These radiant September nights, they sing so rarely.

Does the way light falls on this or that landscape
at sunrise or sunset, on this minute or that
finally pull the plug on the word machine
leaving silence to connect us after all?

Brighton is happening now and without you.
London   Boston   New York   are repeating themselves
            without you.

200,000–10,000 BC   Cwm Nantcol is carved by glaciers.

2613–2495 BC   Mycerinus and his queen are blessed by
                      Egyptian gods.

2005 AD   A postcard from Kew depicting Himalayan
                      rhododendrons passes from you to me,

while years are piling up like clouds behind us,
millions upon millions. Before the stars had names
the earth was spinning on its axis,
the carnivores brought down their prey and devoured it,
the vegetarians grazed on, victims oblivious,
no one was there to notice or take notes.

Just as Mr Jones' ewes graze on without you,
  clinging to the planet's surface
  a skin so thin
  holding a ball of liquid fire and water.

Dear poet dear friend dear optimist,
whose breadth of insight and outsight
made free with a painter's eye.
To explore to testify to clarify
to tell your story or part of it,
as much truth as the truth will bear,
always stopping at the border where language
smudges the lines or draws its own conclusions –
such was your appeal against the monster.

To stand near the summit of Mt Tamalpais
or any real imaginary mountain
looking down on a dazzle of clouds
and know them, those transmutations of fog –
such was the pinnacle you aimed for,
such was the paradise you claimed.
No one but you could experience such perfect joy.

(September 2015)

Lee Harwood's visits to Pwllymarch, our family cottage in Cwm Nantcol, North Wales, were yearly events from about 1990.

Quotations from Lee Harwood's poems:

'finally pull the plug on the word machine' from 'A poem for writers' (*Collected Poems*, Shearsman Books, p. 299).

'clinging to the planet's surface / a skin so thin / holding a ball of liquid fire / and water' ('Sea Journals' 5, *Collected Poems*, p. 240).

A Dream of Guilt

Remembering my mother

When in that dream you censure me,
I wander through a house of guilt.
It has a door – apology –
and windows – smiles. My selves have built
this huge, half-loved neglected place
out of the lintels of your face.

And still I hurt you. Still I – we –
entangle in obscure regret.
Your kind restraint, like stolen money,
weighs on me. I can't forget. I can't forget.
Hushed memories like cobwebs lace
this house too fragile to efface.

Improvisation

In memory of Bernard Roberts, pianist, 1933–2013

A house of fantasy, a house of music
grounded in time and built of trembling air,
a lofty many-sided School of Listening
where players in the rooms above can hear
the music rising from the rooms below,
but those below hear nothing from above.
So, Bach, still counterpointing the foundation,
is banned by a flight of years from hearing Mozart,
and Mozart, for all his gifts, stays locked behind
the singing pillars of his classic forms
as deaf to Beethoven's transcendent range
as Beethoven to Schubert, close yet far.
So Brahms, Schumann, Mendelsohn, Debussy
soar up among the few still listened to,
while thousands in the cobwebbed catacombs,
unheard, are spared the news that they're unheard.

Imagine the topmost floor of such a school.
His spirit could be part of his piano.
Playing it, arms crossed like Brahms,
he guides his listening hands about the keys
as gifts from the composers filter though him.
And though it's true not one of them can hear him,
you'd almost think that playing them, he was them.

A different view? Then let imagination
build for the great musicians an academy,
a timeless concert hall, the sovereign source
of pitch and harmony, to which their souls

return as to a master class, where Beethoven,
his ears restored, advises on the Waldstein,
and J.S. Bach, delighted with his Steinway,
improvises Preludes and Fugues, Book III.
And here – can't you see? – is a burly figure
listening attentively, making a few suggestions,
seating himself at last to perform a definitive
Prelude in C sharp minor –
despite Professor Tovey's fervent muttering,
or Wagner's, amazed to hear a man from Manchester
play like a god despite his English tongue.

Completing the Circle

Remembering Susan Cooper and Anita Jackson

Sea and sky –

Two panels of glass
stretched one above the other,
two panels of blue glass.

Kandinsky. Bach at the organ
tossing sunlight between voices,
some whole, some broken.

The mathematics of colour sings
brave as a rainbow
that rubs itself out against air.

But dying is the water side of waking.
Rainbow is not all.
You can strike light

out of the bruised seventh
of the Dorian scale,
or out of the imaginary curve

that completes the full circle
of a life's yearning
solely at night, beyond eyesight.

Ann Arbor Days, 1947–1950

Remembering Esther Newcomb Goody, 1933-2018

Best friends, we were girls who didn't want to be girls.
Nor, goodness knows, did we want to be boys –
odd creatures, freer than us but not so smart,
with whom, in class, we pleasantly joshed or clashed,
though when it came to dates or high school dances,
they never looked at us or took us out.
Who cared? We were inseparable musketeers
with sword and pen in Esther's garden shed,
tilting with fencing foils or ping pong bats,
writing with pigeon feathers dipped in ink,
swearing faith to friends and death to foes
in pink *Koolade* tossed back in champagne glasses.

I guess we were glad to be us, exclusive, excluded,
avoiding our bodies, disguising our rivalry,
hiding ourselves, protected by make believe before we
threw off our childhoods like clothes on Olivia Avenue
and in nothing but youth and illusion set off for Cambridge –
a diversion for me, for which you wore bridesmaid blue;
a vocation for you in the sweet slum of Shelly Row.
We were always a 'you' and a 'me' in our different Englands.
Our America faces, looking up from our U.S. passports,
now and then whispered, *though I may not feature much
in your self-conception, I'll be there in the mix of
whatever you do and wherever you choose to go.*

It's an accent and voice I recognise, and it comes from
the garden shed. I hear it intoned in a dream I have
of running under elms, over lawns and across the street
to the Newcombs' wrap-around, chocolate-coloured porch.

I knock and ask for Esther. 'No, Esther isn't here.
She's gone off to Ghana for good, you know.' 'For good?'
'For good.' It's her mother Mary I'm talking to,
but the house is empty and dusty. She won't let me in.
'Not Goody but good!' I laugh in my dream.
Then, not in unhappiness, I wake up.

This poem was written at the request of Mary and Rachel Goody for their mother's funeral in Cambridge on the 7th February 2018. The Esther Newcomb I remember best was my closest friend at The University High School, in Ann Arbor, Michigan, before her precocious brilliance got her an early admission to Oberlin College in Ohio. Later we met in Cambridge where Esther was my bridesmaid when I married a Cambridge graduate in 1955. A few years later, she married the anthropologist Jack Goody and became a distinguished anthropologist herself. Their first house in Cambridge was a condemned cottage in Shelly Row, where I remember them in their 'sweet slum' as very happy despite the lack of a proper kitchen or bathroom. Esther and I renewed our friendship in Cambridge during the 1960s, when we introduced out daughters, and later in the 1970s and 80s, before she left to live the greater part of her life in Ghana.

The Day

The day after I die will be lively with traffic. Business
will doubtless be up and doing, fuelled by creative percentages;
the young with their backpacks will be creeping snail-like to school,
closed in communication with their phones. A birth could happen
in an ambulance. A housewife might freak out and take a train to
     nowhere,
but news on *The News* with irrepressible importance will still sweep
everybody into it like tributaries in a continental river system,
irreversible, overwhelming and so virtually taken for granted
that my absence won't matter a bit and will never be noticed.

Unless, of course, enough evidence were preserved to record
the memorable day of my death as the same day all traffic ceased
in the pitiful rubble of Albert Street, to be excavated safely, much later,
by learned aboriginals, who, finding a file of my illegible markings
(together with the skeleton of a sacred cat), were to reconstruct me
as a myth of virtual immortality, along with a tourist view of a typical
street in the late years of the old technological West – a period
they could just be learning to distinguish from the time of the Roman
     wall,
built of stone (so it seemed) long before anything was built of electricity.

Choose to be a Rainbow

> Think about a particular raindrop as a sphere. The sun is
> behind you... and light from it enters the raindrop. At the
> boundary of air with water it is refracted and different wave-
> lengths that make up the sun's light are bent through different
> angles, as in Newton's prism.
>
> RICHARD DAWKINS, *Unweaving the Rainbow*
> (Penguin Books, 1999), p.46

And so to dust? Disperse in the lift of a poem.
Don't let that lean and hungry letter I
Depend on your dust to be forever *am*.
Choose to be rain, illuminate the sky,
Capture the sunlight's slant prismatic glow
And so become immortal every day –
Shattered creator of a changeless show
Ever renewing its need to die away.

Such are our peacock fantasies of heaven –
Keats's angel wing, the immortality
Of Wordsworth's fond imagining. Even
The last light of the end, drawn out or sudden,
Could be filed in raindrops, tears in which to see
Not angels but angles dancing perfectly.

For George Szirtes at seventy

Heartsong

O who could have foretold
That the heart grows old?

W.B. YEATS,
'A Song'

The locked diary of the heart
stores the complete record
in its brisk two-step –
the times when fear or love
made it miss a beat,
sink or leap.

Although it never accuses,
it logs your case exactly,
its archive holds
each crazy wish, each excess,
every instance that has caused it
to soften or harden.

And one day, when perhaps the doctors
come to interpret its scars,
its peaks and troughs,
you, reading over their shoulders,
will see that the heart has remained
as innocent as the Earth itself.

Lullaby

It starts at the brow
moves like a comb
slowly back over the head –
one direction
always – one
definition of home

It is four fingers
threading their way –
soon your eyes will close –
often there comes
a moment when
there is nothing more to say

Unhurried
mildly narcotic
moving in one direction –
behind the ears
or at the nape
it becomes almost hypnotic

It soothes, soothes
moving in one
direction, always one –
quite unaware
of the dark outside
or time racing on

Pas de Trois

(for Grace and Rose)

When on the last day but one
of being thirteen your daughters
turn on the radio and start
to dance side by side
with their long hair flying
and their easy swinging limbs
threading a way that runs
from the Beatles to seventies disco
to straight-backed Irish line-dancing
and though unrehearsed
somehow match each other
in step and turn and delight
expressed in the looks they exchange
and their strong wordless faith
in the beat of the moment
then all three of us know
how lucky it is for some
when on the last day but one
of being thirteen your daughters
tune the kitchen radio
to a station that calls itself *Heart*

Notes on a Fossil Fish

Found in the same vicinity
as the marks of ancient raindrops –
another outrider.
                    Certified
a true likeness of time.

Imprint of only one
on neutral Permian clay,
as if intact.
                    Caudal
and dorsal fins clearly visible.

Likewise, folds of skin
at the disbelieving mouth.
Ghost of a socketed eye.
Back arched.
                    Flank
stippled, partly hatched.
Scales as textured cladding.

Still has real heft.
Survives in its way. Lives
quietly in a backwater
of the mind.
                    Not far from where
I keep Emerson's remark that
language is fossil poetry.

Clues

(for Helen)

The quiver of pik-a-stiks
gleaned on a walk
for you is enough
to unlock entirely
the black and white truth
of the porcupine's life –
its ditch-runs, its habitat,
its way of listening
to passing humans.

You won't take them home,
you say, the solid
little javelins,
but leave them in a pot
for others to imagine
how a porcupine is –
its rattling armour,
its crouch, the angle
of its watchful eye.

And maybe that
is akin to the way
someone might describe
freedom as a bird
or love as a boy
armed with arrows.
Meanwhile, in the dark
a hustling bulk
prepares to take aim.

Giacometti's *Cat*

Its head to body to tail
is one long, mean
horizontal hoisted
on the spindly twin trestles
of its best feet forward

A nerve-bundle fused in bronze
it lives apart, locked
in a trance of stealth
as it probes the air ahead
taking nothing for granted

Zigzag

I love the word's
obliquity, its insistence
on heading off
in two directions
while aiming at a third –
its swoop and verve.

It thrives in the in
and out of traffic,
favours the player
with the ball, and the skier
slaloming down
in a spray of ice.

I have seen it flourish
under the signatures
of the famous, or the track
of the boat beating
to windward – always told
in guises and angles.

And only by following
each turn and retort
of the chalk path
lacing the hillside
can you imagine
a way through.

Moths Queuing

Their fluttering is fraught
as if, like us, they know
what is in wait, how time
and failure consume us *as it were*
a moth fretting a garment –
and wield their names like blazons –
the dingy and orange footmen,
the scorched wings, the brimstones,
the flame shoulders.
                And this
is only a start: further back,
white ermines, square-spots,
yellow-barred brindles, clouded
silvers, ghost-moths, even
the small phoenix, are all
pressing forward, with furious
imperative beating, beating,
clamorous for the light.

Thinking of Steve Sims

Between faith and words, you discerned
so little distance that you hardly needed
to mind the gap – yet you were always
mindful of others. You attended to life
with a cocked ear.

Between text and context, you sensed
a deeply humming connection able
to outflank any ill, a language that valued
rough gutturals as much as it did
the smooth run of vowels.

Between love and wisdom, you made
your own brave, slightly rumpled way
to where I see you now, on the brink
of nirvana – and serene, free of pain, smiling.
Above all, smiling.

Smoke-rings

Perfectly round or sometimes oval,
each one miraculous, and even more so
when one of many mouthed in succession,
they move like bowled hoops, with the same
slight wobble till, too soon, they lose
definition and fade to almost nothing.

The best smoke-rings I've ever seen
were blown in Kenya by a teacher from England
who retired to Malindi, impulsively buying
a house not far from the dark glitter
of mica on the beach, and the sighs of the ocean.

Amused at first, in time he found it
less and less easy to wait for the trunk
he said was mislaid on the voyage out
long ago. And time was extreme –
the ants trekking to and from sugar-grains,
the gecko at its station on the *pisé* wall.

In the morning, dealing with household tasks;
once, a whole day to replace a bathplug.
In the afternoon, the crossword, sleep,
then gin, backgammon. In the whining night,
groping to trap another dose of Mogadon.

Words were at least a defence, a deflection –
he liked them full, orotund, able
to speak for themselves and for him, to whom utterance
was also disownment. He saw them off
as smoke-rings, with a limp wave of the arm
that was half farewell, half a conjuror's pride.

The habit became impossible to break –
and the last smoke-ring he ever blew me
read: *My health is very good*
apart from all the things that are wrong with me.
It wobbles there, never fading completely.

Birdcall

Remembering Helen Dunmore

Eight days on, in the morning dusk
of four o'clock, the summons
of the blackbird's liquid song
loops up from the garden
three floors below

It conjures the image of you looking out
from your own tall house, delighted
at the bird's-eye view across
the river and the city backed
by marching hills

Most of all, the river's coming
and going, with its endless traffic
of boats, its swarm of detail,
and the changes of light dinting
the surface with dazzle

...And the image of the bird itself, close
to our freckled foxgloves or the gatepost,
black plumage offset
by its crocus-yellow bill
and enquiring eye

How you cherished the world! And I see,
when abruptly the song stops,
how the bird has been calling
attention not to itself,
but the silence following

Female Head, about 1525

Our lady of the liminal –
witness at her back the margins of
the unruly forest,
and the real focus of her regard
being offstage.

But the heart of the story is locked
in the ghost of her gaze – its candour,
the early signs
of grief, a drift to the verge
where hope wavers.

And everywhere, time on the make –
in the darkening turquoise of the sky,
the slow swell
of the trees, the craquelure moving up
to infect her soft features.

Four Late van Goghs

Undergrowth

Tufts of light flicker
on its low, sea-green swell
like an old exile's
memories of home

Snagged but forceful, it is
past clear defining,
with nowhere to go,
nothing to be done –

Will trap you as you attempt
to tread it down: is waiting
for the next bombed city,
the next ruin

Autumn Walk

October – the light
curdling, all the sheen
sucked out
of plant and tree

The last of the leaves
have become sketchy darts
hurled by the wind
groundwards like chaff

You know the name
of the man in the blue coat
walking so awkwardly.
This is life, not art.

Umber reaches up
from the earth's shadows.
Pale grey paths
lead back and on.

Asylum Garden, December

The tree dismembered
at head height
has found new ways
of striving skyward

between two bare
and empty benches
the only discourse
is absence, silence

– and a far figure
is walking, dwarfed
by wind-racked trees,
a sky that won't settle

whichever way
he looks or goes,
walls, or figures
watching from the terrace

and quite out of reach
the impossibly blue
distant hilltop
edged with red

Tree Roots

It has come to this –
earth and sky
dissolving together
to bone, dust-dry

no sense to be made
of the *bonsai* dreams
greenly clinging
to what might have been

except by seeing
in one man's witness
how truth matters more,
beauty less

A Wedding Photo from 1975

(for David and Tina Pease)

Much more than the riot of hair
it is your leaning together, and the flourish
of both your right arms half raised
and waving that claim the viewer's attention.

These are not the urgent gestures
of the charioteer as he reins in
or the sailor hauling hard on the sheet,
but of energy released, joy on the loose.

Smiling, you have broken free from the threshold
where someone is watching as you spill headlong
into the future. Time seems simply
the marker from which you happened to set out.

And even now the eye, as it follows
the curve of your gestures into history, keeps
imprinted on the retina this image of delight,
the parabola of the dream's momentum.

Triggers

Increasingly rare, but still
every so often, from
a thunderous motorbike
or an ancient car, the whiff
of leaded fuel
triggers two faithful extracts
held in the synaptic records –

the child's simple wonder
at the sheen of spilt petrol
in its peacock puddle,
the fuzzy iridescence
of green, blue,
yellow, pink, mauve
spread on the dark tarmac

– and, from the chickling warmth
of an uncle's dim barn,
hemmed in among
prickly haybales, and flying
a winged letter A
from its bonnet, the old saloon,
its ineffable scent of leather

Three Time-signatures

(for John Lucas at 80)

1 *Prototype Electric Bicycle*
(Ben Bowden, 1946)

An artist's impression
of itself it has
all the gloss
of the quite unreal –
could aptly lean against
an architect's dream
among unbuilt buildings
play-doh trees
model people

Impossibly sleek
in its silver casing
it shimmers eerily
ahead of its time –
but quite as real
as any archetype
produced in the mind's
workshop of the possible

2 *Helmet Head No. 1*
(Maquette, Henry Moore, 1950)

Nothing more threatening
than the threat spoken softly
or less ready
to compromise

Its bronze is perhaps
not auto-immune
attacking the head
it was meant to defend

Nothing more alert
than the epiglottal
or uvular protusion
half-hidden inside

Nib or spearhead
waiting

3 *Crown Merton Double Saucepan*
(c. 1960s)

Two semi-circles
fitted inside
a full circle –
two handles, two lids

Some archaeologist's
find, no doubt,
aluminium, ancient,
with a fake recent date

or Babushka reductions
an insider's joke
double and double
a conjuror's trick

or austerity kitchenware
designed by Magritte
ce n'est ni une casserole
ni une pipe

Briefing Model for D-day

Will not would
Shall not should
Juno here
and here, Sword.
Beach-head not beach.
This is as good
as it gets.

Keep wading.
Be aware
of enfilade.
Move forward.
Attack not defence.

At the fringe of the sea
the slopes and dunes
are shown in relief.
Phase one
will end at noon.

It won't be quite
as neat on the ground
it never is
but believe you me
the model is sound
This is as good
as it gets

Woodlice and Earthworm

The rockery stone, dislodged,
exposes a seethe
of grey lozenges
in pure panic

Everywhere, anywhere they scramble,
desperate to get away
from whatever it is
that has blown their cover

And then the earthworm, sliced
by the spade – mucous,
blood-bruised, naked,
halfway to transparent

Chopped in half, it just waves
each hurt bit
curling away
to alleged restoration

And all this was before
the child had ever been stung
by a wasp, or read about
snakes in gardens

Belonging

We learn to belong to our name –
after all, it follows us
everywhere, like a shadow,
even from language to language.

As once it followed my father
until, in his need to belong,
from shame or for love he decided
to trade it in for a new one.

How well he learnt to wear
his new cloak, to answer to
his new name! Under its cover
in the end he made off.

And today, a letter from one
of my German cousins, close
on the death of her mother who,
she writes, *spent her life helping others.*

Of course, she adds, *you*
belong to us too. And even
all these years later, something
for which I have no name, snaps.

Cut Flowers

Yellow roses
still in tight bud
and lavish, they
sway forward,
a crowd craning
for a better view.

There is, though, only
a bare circle
of soil cleared
enough to allow
the passage of a casket
with its cargo of sift.

Nearby, a basket
with sweet peas
to scatter like confetti –
mauve, red,
white, they float down
to the rim of the dark.

The moment can hardly
contain the riches
of a life well lived
as nurse, doctor,
wife, mother –
and, always, a believer.

Even when ordered
like her fellow trainees
to dissect corpses
emaciated,
branded with a number –
still a believer.

She would have us wait
for that naked ground
to heal enough
to take new growth,
the uncut flowers
of the next spring.

Shine

It was all curtailed by then –
your home rendered to a home,
your car to a small cheque,
your love of travel to a short
walk in the garden: your furniture
to what would fit into one room.

So where did it come from, that radiance
which took possession of your features?
Your gaze was shine, all shine
and seemed to fix on something
out of sight. You smiled
as if greeting a guest.

An ecstasy that bordered
on rapture, it had nothing
to say – if spoken to
you were speechless, not so much
astonished as taken up
with something else altogether.

At the point of no return
perhaps, with simply nothing
more to be said, even
to your children. You spent the whole
of your last week in that glow
and did not speak again.

Triptych

1

Beyond Elysium Lodge
the numbered and lettered acres
go on and on
sky-wide measures of absence:
with a great mound of bare
bulldozed earth, puddles
of yesterday's rain
stopped in its red tracks.

Truth without beauty, unkempt,
the stumps of broken
crosses, skewed stones,
fallen limbs of evergreen.

Sorrow here is the light
that streams in black and gold
from the polished marble
of an outsize new headstone:
disbelief, a drenched cluster
of teddies, wizened balloons
out of breath,
helpless choked words.

And near the fenced-off chapels,
like random clues – syringes,
bottles, a squirrel
scurrying, a hopping crow.

2

Their stone tents stretch across
the swell of the slopes –
the regular troops who serve for ever,
lieutenant lustrum, yeoman year,
major minute, subaltern second,
the whole rhetorical army drilling
in overloaded tropes.

The maisonettes of failing memory
are crumbling seriatim,
their cankered façades, sagged, have become
tablets on which near-crazed explorers
record their baffled failure to locate
Morrison's grave. *Where the fuck
are you, Jim?*

And where amongst others are Piaf, Proust,
Apollinaire,
Bizet, Callas, Chabrol, Éluard,
Isadora Duncan, Oscar Wilde,
Balzac, Colette, Kreutzer, La Fontaine,
Chopin, Corot, Daumier, Delacroix,
and Poquelin *dit* Molière?

With the gentlest of touches on the shoulder, death
assumes the guise
of a great romance, a darkness ahead
so softly lined that it almost seems
a logical end to the cobbled sunlight
and the pediments from which a final trill
of avid birdsong rises.

3

Domino effects
the dead fallen flat
end to end
tamped down
under heavy lids
of millstone grit

Prise any up
to find hard labour
warp and weft
working together
to fashion the most
that dust could become

The nearby buildings
reel back
chimneys gushing
fast smoke –
grief can hardly
get a purchase

In the valley, where
the swart river
runs on regardless,
the creamy faces
of small-town clocks
parody the moon

At a Concert

We do not often converse
with the dead, or they with us,
and then on their terms only
or when we least expect it –
as at an autumn concert
of medieval songs
at Loiras-du-Bosc, in the simple
space of the whitewashed church.

How that confident mezzo,
with her flashing eyes, conjured
those cansos! With coiling gestures
of her arms, halfway to dancing,
and her free to and fro walking
as she sang, then softly tapped
the tambourine held to her ear.
Whatever it was she heard
was a secret she had to share.

It was something more than the sighs
of those courtly arranged non-marriages
the troubadours loved – something older
and wilder that she seemed to know,
brought down from the scant topsoil
of the high limestone plateau.
More a tone than a voice,
a held note that carried
the pathos, joy and rancour
of lives barely sustainable.

At the end – applause, dispersal.
The road makes its twisting way
through a country of sandy soil
rife with loose stones, far too many
to count. Then, a small field

of newly planted olive trees,
their silver-green leaves imprinted
on the twilight. A brusque wind
frisks some roadside bushes.
A hint of rain. Slowly
the present reclaims the ground.

Masquerade

ANTONIO: In sooth I know not why I am so sad.

The Merchant of Venice, I. 1

I blush to think how, denying
my friend's suggestion so quickly,
I gave myself away – and still
the pulse of his voice beats
in my head: *Why then, Antonio,*
you are in love.

In truth, at that point the truth
was no clearer than the city itself
in the weak light of winter,
shrouded and shelved somewhere
uncertain, between the flows
of sky and sea.

And then, the waking dream
in the murk of an alley which ended
where the water lapped greenly
at stone – just as the wind
veered, the three masquers
who appeared from nowhere.

One with the lined features
of profit and loss, the trade-off
of wrecking storms and the calm
of ships laden with spices
nuzzling the wharfs. A smile
that kept on smiling.

And one with a face carved
in the spitting image of hate –
brittle with rage, intent
on tracking down a scapegoat
even if that should come to
pure self-harm.

But the third masquer, shouldering
a patched old lute – he
was the one I could not evade,
who had me at the mercy.
I was his eye-baby, caught
in the compass of his gaze.

At that moment I saw
how to plot the true
course from A to B
whatever the dangers – how
to become, in joy and terror,
Antonio in love.

Seafaring

(for George Szirtes at 70)

The bill of lading is hardly
a legible account of the truth
to be smuggled through – and no
yellow flag is run up
for the nicety of customs clearance

Each vessel has to find
its own track across
the wild welter of the sea –
and must manage its own cargo
that is always in danger of shifting

And each is a bucking entry
in a rich thesaurus that harbours,
for example, coracles, dinghies,
luggers, caravels, clippers,
steamers, an ark – even

A child's boat launched
at dusk in a dream of Europe
and *frêle comme un papillon de mai* –
one among too many
new-found translations of sorrow

And though the binnacled compass
swings crazily between
never, soon, eventually
and whenever, its directions
can still hold good in time –

As sombre or playful readings
that reify the random
and make the voyage out
not just one of discovery
but of homing to recognition

Kepler's Epitaph

I used to measure the skies, now I measure the shadows of Earth.
Although my mind was sky-bound, the shadow of my body lies here.

JOHANNES KEPLER

There is more to Earth
than epitaphs allow
with their cold comparing
of mind and body
earth and air.

Summer sears
the chalk paths
beneath your feet.
The silence of the mountains
swells with heat.

In measures of meaning
so much depends
on order and art –
each zigzag word
playing its part.

Even the moon
lifting above
the cypresses owes
its bright coinage
to the Earth's own glow.

Sentences for Vivaldi's *Gloria*

[following No. 3, Laudamus te]

In the salt brightness of the lagoon, glory
In the worn cities and the hills, praise
In the local weather of love, adoration
In heart and mind, the working muscle of thankfulness

[following No. 7, Domini fili]

In the slow hours of reckoning, pain
In time, the sense of time misjudged
In riches locked away, the failure of love
In every war, the simple cruelty of the strong

[following No. 10, Qui sedes ad dexteram]

In help and laughter, a grounded hope
In spite of nightmares, the dream of grace
In singers' exposed voices, trust
In the pulse of music, the quickening trumpets of glory

Instances

You see only close to
that the bed of the old watercourse
is lined with oval stones
smoother than the water itself

Flares of rust and algae,
chatoyant, they wind skeins
of bright green, orange, brown
under the fall of the flow

Rinsed clear of history,
they match the precise with the almost
abstract, as might a reduced
map of a whole universe

*

A single casement
is enough to draw
the slow-shifting
alto-cumulus
to the proper limit
of close focus

The cloud billows
but stays contained –
one framed instance
suggesting to the mind
the full extent
of the unseen sky

Just so, the heart
reads into
a sudden blush
or the way an angel,
kneeling, takes
centre stage

Sea Pictures

As a boy, when the Odeon stood in for the ocean
I saw for myself, in black and white,
just how welcoming the water could be –
how easily a body tipped up
slid from its canvas shroud with never
a murmur of a splash.

*

From the swimmer's unsteady eye level
the waves race away ahead, each crest
as it flares and flows swallowing the land,
each trough in its brief slack
allowing it to show. The deckled shoreline
comes and goes.

*

At the hour when the candle burns blue
a man is wading out, each step
more and more dogged by heaviness.
The sea resists him. He needs it to help,
to take him in, rinse him clean
of every sorrow.

*

The idea of the sea is intense light
holding above the network of hedges
in the last high field: it could be nothing else.
One final effort – the weary hoplites
clear their throats, get ready to shout
Thalassa! Thalassa!

*

The sea laps to shore like a well-trained pet,
the water clear enough to cast shadows
on its smooth ground. Or snaps a mast,
shouts at you, has the sails flogging
like pumped-up ghosts. Never look to the sea
for consistency.

*

On a summer night, when the salt breeze
blows steady and warm, it sometimes happens
as it twists low past riding hulls,
with the land shrunk into darkness, that the sea
will relax and throw the whole sky
wide open.

Recognition

Once, I thought
nothing could be sadder
than to spend a lifetime
paddling at the brink
of your real self

Now, I think
that saddest of all
is not to recognise
that figure stumbling
along the shore

Mayflower

Out from Plymouth, braced by the westerlies,
the ship gathers way, taking the brunt
of the swell, foam flaring at its prow.

Laden with stores, with its mixed human cargo
of faith and fear, aversion and love,
it is steering for hope and a vision of home,
but for now must focus on the brute struggle
to weather storms, and learn how to ride
the pitch and fall of the juddering seas.

Time enough later to confront the conflicts
landfall will bring – and, all these years on,
for us to ponder our own voyaging.

We explore in the round, with a view
of the Earth seen from space, the apparent calm
of its settlements – but we know too its urgent need
for renewal, for the oceans to be cleared of rubble
and the air made good, for forests to thrive
and every creature have its living.

For us also it is too late
to plead innocence – yet still we must hope
to drop anchor within hailing distance of wisdom.

Rainer Maria Rilke's *Ninth Duino Elegy*

Why, when it comes to living out
the mortal span in the guise of a laurel, a bit darker
than any other shade of green, with little serrations
along each leaf-edge (like a benign breeze) – why then
the human imperative – while outflanking fate,
still to long for fate?...
            Oh, *not* because happiness *exists*,
that reckless gain before an imminent loss.
Not out of curiosity, or to exercise the heart,
which *might* also inhere in the laurel.....

But because hereness means much, and because it seems
all that is here and now needs us, all that is ephemeral
and so strangely involved with us. Us, the most ephemeral of all.
Once, everything only *once*. *Once* and nevermore. And we, too,
once. Never again. But to have existed
this *once*, even if only *once*:
to have been *of the Earth*, this seems irrevocable.

And so we drive ourselves on, striving for achievement,
striving to embody it in our simple hands,
in a gaze of greater intensity, in the speechless heart.
Strive to become it. – To whom shall we give it? Preferable
to keep hold of it all for ever... But, alas! What can be carried over
into that other sphere? Not the world as we see it here,
so arduously learnt, and no earthly event. Not one.
The pangs of pain, then. Most of all, then, weightiness,
and so, the long apprenticeship of love – so, only
the untellable. But later,
under the stars, no matter: *they* are *better* untellable.
For even from the brink of the mountain slope, the traveller
carries down to the valley, not a handful of soil, untellable to anyone,
but rather a won word, pure, the yellow and blue
gentian. The point of our *hereness* is, perhaps, to utter: House,

Bridge, Fountain, Gate, Jug, Fruit Tree, Window –
at most: Column, Tower.... yet to utter, don't misunderstand me,
oh to utter them in *such* a way as things
could never themselves intend. Is it not the secretive cunning
of this withdrawn world, when it urges lovers on,
that each and every thing should delight in their feeling?
Threshold: what it might mean to two
lovers that they should, however slightly, scuff the already
worn threshold for themselves, after the many before them
and before those who come after...., slightly.

Here is the time of the tellable, *here* its home.
Speak and bear witness. More than ever
things once available to experience are falling apart, for
what ousts and supersedes them is purblind action,
action to the point at which the surface crust easily fragments,
the moment it outgrows containment and seeks new frontiers.
Between the hammers it persists,
our heart, like the tongue
between the teeth, which still
utters its praise nonetheless.

To the angel praise the world, but not the untellable one,
you cannot impress *him* with your elevated feelings;
in the cosmos, where he feels more feelingly, you are a novice.
Therefore show him what is simple, shaped from one generation
to the next, and exists as ours, within our reach and focus.
Tell him of things. He will stand in renewed awe, as you once stood
at the rope-maker's in Rome, or the potter's by the Nile. Show him
how joyous a thing can be, how innocent and our own,
how even the protest of grief resolves purely as a figure,
plays its part as a thing, or dies into a thing – how, beyond,
it serenely eludes the violin. And such things, nourished
by mortality, understand your praise of them: transient, they entrust
a saving grace to us, the most transient of all.
Wanting us to change them utterly, in the secrecy of the heart,
into – ah, endlessly – ourselves ! Whoever we may finally be.

Is it not this, Earth, that you desire: to arise
in us *invisibly*? – Is it not your dream
some day to be invisible? – Earth! invisible!
What, if not this transformation, is your urgent task?
Earth, dear one, I desire it. Oh believe me, it would take
no more of your spring-times to win me over – *one*,
ah, a single one produces a rush of blood.
Anonymously I came down on your side long ago.
Always you were in the right, and death in its intimacy
is your sacred inspiration.

Look, I am alive. How so? Neither childhood nor the future
is dwindling..... Existence beyond measure
wells up in my heart.

Asphodels

Always waiting at the margin
Spikes of yellow or white
Persephone's garland –
Homer spread them lavishly
Over the meadows where
Dead Achilles strode
Easily across the
Last of the yielding earth,
Stepping away for ever

NOTES

At the Equinox (22)
In the Anglican calendar, St Michael and all Angels, at the time of the autumn equinox, is one of two dates in the year marked for the ordination of priests and deacons.

Sarabande (27)
This is a response to the fourth movement of the fourth of J.S. Bach's suites for solo cello.

Triptych (59)
The three cemeteries that make up the triptych are: Upper Cemetery, Exeter; Père Lachaise, Paris; and Heptonstall, West Yorkshire.

Masquerade (64)
The number three is not just the tally of masquers, but is embedded in the play in a variety of ways. Antonio-Bassanio-Portia is in many respects a triad (however much implied rather than explicit); there are three caskets; three thousand ducats is the sum of the loan; three is the number of Antonio's argosies that make it to their home port.

This links in my mind with the idea of the Trinity, as well as the three-part parabola of sin – forgiveness – redemption. In the context of the New Testament, the inevitable recall is of the encounter on the road to Emmaus, and Eliot's summoning of that occasion in *The Waste Land*: 'Who is the third who walks always beside you?' ('What the Thunder said').

These triform aspects have found their way (but identified only in the wake of composition) into three-stress lines – all, apart from the final line of each verse. There are three syllables in the poem's title, and the total number of lines is a multiple of three.

The poem springs off from the opening words of the play; but also, albeit in a contrary direction, from Antonio's comment

in II. 6, line 65 – 'No masque tonight, the wind is come about'
– thought by some commentators to be the residue of a fuller
masque scene.

Sentences for Vivaldi's *Gloria* (68)

I have kept these sentences short. Syntactically and rhythmically,
they share the same pattern: in writing them I had the Psalms
in mind. Each group of sentences takes up the mood of the
preceding or following sections of music. Thus the first group
echoes the notes of praise of the *Gloria*'s first three sections;
the second anticipates the penitential and redemptive elements
of sections 8-10; and the final group, weighing darkness against
light, is a bridge to the affirmation of the two final choruses.